This book~
belongs~
~~to...~~ ~~____~~
F Lin

Pokémon™

Johto Region Field Guide

WELCOME TO JOHTO!

NEW BARK TOWN

New Bark Town's motto, "Where the winds of new beginnings blow," is a perfect description for the town because it's the place where all Pokémon Trainers in Johto begin their adventures. The first stop for brand new Trainers is Professor Elm's Laboratory, while experienced Pokémon Trainers from other lands should check in at New Bark Town's Pokémon Center.

THE ELECTABUZZ

Some people dismiss New Bark Town's baseball team, the Electabuzz, as inferior to other squads such as the Starmies and Magikarp. That doesn't matter to the team's devoted fanbase, which includes the entire family of a Pokémon Trainer named Casey. They are optimistic that the Electabuzz will finish at the top of the standings every year.

PROFESSOR ELM

Professor Elm runs the Elm Laboratory in New Bark Town, and is responsible for providing new Trainers with their first partner Pokémon. He is easily distracted while working on his research, and has been known to launch into lengthy speeches on Pokémon-related topics.

He was a student of Professor Oak (if you ask Professor Elm, he will insist that he was Oak's top student). But now he regards his old teacher as a rival. Professor Elm's first paper was an analysis of hybridized communicative faculties of Pokémon, but he has changed his focus to unusual Pokémon abilities.

ELM LABORATORY

Professor Elm's laboratory in New Bark Town is where he conducts his research. It's also where new Trainers pick up their first partner Pokémon from the Johto region.

JOHTO FIRST PARTNER POKÉMON

Brand new Trainers in Johto must choose one of three different Pokémon. **Chikorita** is a Grass-type Pokémon, which can evolve into Bayleef, then Meganium. **Cyndaquil** is a Fire-type Pokémon, which can evolve into Quilava, then Typhlosion. **Totodile** is a Water-type Pokémon, which can evolve into Croconaw, then Feraligator.

New Bark Town Pokémon Center

A visit to the Pokémon Center in New Bark Town is a requirement for Trainers who want to compete in the Johto League. There's no entry fee, so all you need to do is speak with Nurse Joy. After signing up, your goal is to earn badges by defeating eight Gym Leaders. Violet City hosts the closest Gym to New Bark Town, making it an ideal initial destination to win your first Gym badge.

NEW BARK TOWN TO VIOLET CITY

The road from New Bark Town to Violet City takes you through the wilderness and a few cities. The city nearest to New Bark Town is Florando.

Leafy Forest

Not far outside New Bark Town is a forest watched over by the rangers of the Forest and Wildlife Bureau. Its Pokémon inhabitants include Heracross and Butterfree, which work together to feed on tree sap, and a colony of Pinsir that don't get along with the other Pokémon.

Amberite Valley

Beyond the leafy forest is a wide valley that's a source of amberite, a gemstone so precious it was once worn by royalty. Trained Donphan are able to sniff out the amberite, which is then sold to craftspeople who create jewelry and statues.

Forest of Illusions

Mischievous Gengar and Haunter use illusions to startle and confuse anyone trying to pass through this forest not far from Florando. To travel safely, seek out Hagatha and Nagatha. These twin sisters rent their Hoothoot for their Foresight ability, which disrupts the illusions of the Ghost-type Pokémon. Anyone who attempts to follow the trails through the forest without properly trained Pokémon may become lost for days!

FLORANDO'S POKÉMON EXHIBITION

The Pokémon Exhibition is a giant, outdoor
Pokémon entertainment festival that takes
place every year. Trainers from all over the
world travel to Florando with their Pokémon
to show off a unique talent and compete for the
trophy that is awarded to the winning act.

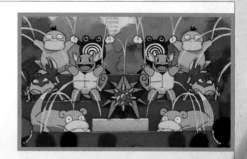

Catallia City

Not far from Florando is Catallia City. Over
one hundred years ago the Black Arachnid, a
legendary cat burglar, and his Meowth partner
terrorized the city. There were recent rumors
about a new Black Arachnid attempting to
break into the mayor's home, but it turned out
to be a group of imposters.

9

SPINARAK

Instead of the commonly used Growlithe, Officer Jenny in Catallia City works with **Spinarak**, the String Spit Pokémon. This partnership goes back more than 100 years, when a Spinarak helped with the capture of the Black Arachnid.

The residents of Cherrygrove City are protective of the local Quagsire population. No one is allowed to battle or capture wild Quagsire because they help identify clean water for the city's use. Every year, the Quagsire gather round objects and take them to Blue Moon Falls for a celebration.

CELEBRATION AT BLUE MOON FALLS

While it may seem odd to visitors, the citizens of Cherrygrove City are overjoyed when the Quagsire begin to take their round belongings. They know everything will be released later from the top of Blue Moon  Falls and float back to Cherrygrove City. An item taken and returned by the Quagsire means the owner will have a year of good luck. The last item recovered from the river is thought to bring its fortunate owner the most luck of all.

LEDYBA

Also known as the Five Star Pokémon, a group of **Ledyba** has been trained to pollenate and harvest the apple trees at an orchard between Cherrygrove City and Violet City.

VIOLET CITY

Violet City and the areas just outside it are a Pokémon fan's dream location. Inside the city are a Pokémon academy and a Gym where experienced Trainers can earn the Zephyr Badge.

NURSE BLISSEY

The Pokémon Center in Happy Town, a suburb of Violet city, has a surprise staff member. Typically, Chansey helps Nurse Joy at Pokémon Centers but in Happy Town that role is filled by **Blissey**, the Happiness Pokémon.

Pokémon Academy and Sprout Tower

The Pokémon academy is run by Earl Dervish, the principal and dance instructor, and Miss Priscilla, who teaches the students about Pokémon and how to be a Trainer. Just like the Pokémon they're studying, the students in the class all have their own personalities. Most are simply curious but watch out for aggressive students. They have been known to try to steal Pokémon from other Trainers!

Not far from the academy is Sprout Tower, a popular destination for Pokémon Trainers traveling to Violet City. Sprout Tower is named for its unusual central support beam, which sways back and forth like a Bellsprout.

Violet Gym

The Gym in Violet City is a tall, purple spiral tower with many windows on it. Battles against Falkner, the Gym Leader, take place in the tower's rooftop arena. During matches, members of the Gym chant in unison, to support their leader.

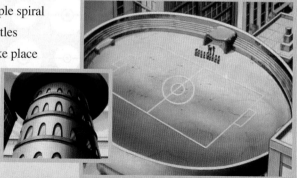

FALKNER

It's not surprising that Violet Gym's Leader uses Flying-type Pokémon exclusively. Since he was a little boy, he's dreamed of flying. Falkner's ambition is to be known as the finest Flying-type Pokémon Trainer that ever lived. He uses a hang glider in order to be closer to his Flying-type Pokémon.

He is a fierce competitor who bristles at the assumption that Flying-types can't defeat Electric-types in battle. However, he holds no grudges against Trainers who defeat him. He hands over a Zephyr Badge and wishes them good luck on their continued journey through Johto.

FALKNER'S POKÉMON

In battle, Falkner sticks with a trio of Normal- and Flying-type Pokémon. **Hoothoot** uses Tackle and Peck. **Dodrio**'s moves include Agility, Fury, Drill Peck, and Tri Attack. **Pidgeot** has employed the Whirlwind, Agility, Wing Attack, and Quick Attack moves during battle.

VIOLET CITY TO AZALEA TOWN

From Violet City, the next closest Gym is in Azalea Town, which is a good distance away. The road winds through a number of cities, forests, rivers, and valleys, which means you should be on the lookout for a plethora of Pokémon along the way.

Charicific Valley

Its full name is the Charicific Valley Natural Reserve and it's off limits to tourists! The entrance is marked with Charizard statues carved from stone and it's difficult to reach. Almost all the Charizard in the valley are wild, but one named Charla works with Liza, the lone human in the valley.

Charicific Valley is a training ground where Charizard go to learn new attacks and hone their abilities against other Charizard. The Charizard in Charicific Valley have lived in peace for thousands of years, and the greatest Charizard in history have come from there.

SUNFLORA FESTIVAL

Bloomingvale is famous for sunny weather and the Sunflora Festival, a big celebration held every year. The festival's showcase event is a competition to determine the best Sunflora smile. The winner of the competition receives a trophy and a year's supply of instant noodles.

Trainers from Bloomingvale are known to go to extremes to gain an advantage for the competition. One Trainer applies overnight mud masks to their Sunflora, in order to reduce wrinkles. Others try tanning and vigorous exercise. Sonrisa, a recent contest winner, claimed her Sunflora needed only fresh water and sunlight.

HOPPIP

A weather station between Bloomingvale and Azalea Town is run by a young meteorologist named Mariah. She uses **Hoppip** to help her learn about the weather. Hoppip, the Cottonweed Pokémon, are light enough to be carried away by the wind. Mariah observes and records the number of Hoppip that float away in the wind, which allows her to predict upcoming weather conditions.

Parker's Toy Shop

A city between Bloomingvale and Azalea Town is home to Mr. Parker's toy shop, which is dedicated to a local hero, Gligarman. For years, he has worked with a Gligar. Recently, a new heroine named Gligirl, has joined Gligarman's battle for truth and defense of the weak.

GLIGAR

While **Gligar**, the Fly Scorpion Pokémon, are known to be temperamental and dislike humans, one formed a bond with Gligarman and Gligirl, helping them to fight crime.

MAREEP FESTIVAL

This annual celebration includes rides, shows, and competitions exclusively featuring Mareep, the Wool Pokémon. The people take pride in the quality of the wool produced by their Mareep, claiming it's the best in the world. Items made with the wool are expensive, so there must be some truth to their claim.

Muramasa's Dojo

Muramasa was one of the top Trainers of his day, but he turned his focus toward training Trainers who wished to become elite. Muramasa's training center draws young Trainers from all over the world, who wish to strengthen themselves and their Pokémon.

SCIZOR

Scizor, the Scissor Pokémon, is the Evolution of Scyther. Scizor is fast and uses large claws in battle. Muramasa's Scizor, Masamune, is so fast that it earned the nickname the Crimson Streak.

AZALEA TOWN

The citizens of Azalea Town are fiercely protective of the local Slowpoke population. Citizens revere Slowpoke so much, even accidentally stepping on a Slowpoke's tail is enough to anger an entire mob against you!

The source of honor and respect for the Dopey Pokémon is a local folktale set four hundred years in the past, when the town was saved from a devastating drought by yawning Slowpoke. As a token of appreciation the people of Azalea Town built the Slowpoke Well, which is also known as Rainmaker's Rest, just outside the town. A more recent drought was brought to end in the same way. The Slowpoke gathered above the Slowpoke Well, and yawned just before a heavy rain began.

KURT

A man from Azalea Town, Kurt had been studying the Slowpoke during the recent drought. Kurt is also a well-known Poké Ball expert who makes custom Poké Balls from Apricorns. He lives with his granddaughter and apprentice, Maizie. She runs errands for him, and has become knowledgeable about Apricorns and Apricorn trees.

POKÉ BALLS FROM APRICORN TREES

The fruit of Apricorn trees come in seven colors: white, red, blue, black, pink, green, and yellow. Poké Balls created from Apricorn have special qualities that set them apart from regular Poké Balls.

Each color of Apricorn Poké Ball has its own name and specific use. Green Apricorns become Friend Balls. Red Apricorns become Level Balls. White Apricorns become Fast Balls, for catching Pokémon that can run away quickly. Pink Apricorns become Love Balls, which work best when trying to catch Pokémon of different gender. Yellow Apricorns become Moon Balls, for catching Pokémon that use Moon Stones to evolve. Blue Apricorns become Lure Balls, which are good for catching Water Pokémon. Black Apricorns become Heavy Balls, which are really good for catching Pokémon that are heavy.

PINECO

Many Pokémon of Azalea Town protect the groves of Apricorn trees so they aren't overharvested, which would damage the local environment. **Pineco**, the Bagworm Pokémon, is one such Pokémon. When startled, Pineco use Self-Destruct with explosive results.

Azalea Gym

The Azalea Gym was built in a forest. The interior looks more like a garden than a typical Pokémon Gym, but that's what makes it the perfect habitat for Bug Pokémon.

The arena inside Azalea Gym is filled with trees. The trees provide a mobility advantage for Pokémon like Spinarak, which can swing between the trees on their webs.

BUGSY

Bugsy thinks Bug Pokémon are the best Pokémon in the world. He's a confident Gym Leader who trains his Pokémon to be fast. He always saves his best Pokémon for last in Gym battles and encourages all of his Pokémon during a fight, even when they fail to win their match.

He trained his Scyther to use its Swords Dance move to deflect Fire-type attacks, which are a Bug-type Pokémon's weakness. If you manage to defeat Bugsy, expect compliments on your skill while he awards the Hive Badge.

BUGSY'S POKÉMON

Bugsy's team is a trio of Bug-type Pokémon. **Metapod** uses Harden and Tackle. **Spinarak** is a Bug- and Poison-type with the String Shot and Poison Sting moves. **Scyther,** a Bug- and Flying-type Pokémon, uses Double Team, Slash, Fury Cutter, and Swords Dance.

AZALEA TOWN TO GOLDENROD CITY

Like much of Johto, the uninhabited land between cities is mostly forests but there's also a large cave system. The cities and towns between Azalea Town and Goldenrod City, which is the home of the next closest Pokémon Gym, offer varied Pokémon events.

Ilex Forest

Not far from Azalea Town is the Ilex Forest, where the trees grow thick. There's a Pokémon Center in the forest, as well as a shrine where locals leave food offerings to the spirit that watches over the forest. The purified charcoal made from the Ilex Forest's trees is famous around the world. The best quality charcoal is made by Trainers who use Pokémon to cut down trees and burn the wood.

Palmpona

Palmpona is home to an annual festival known as the Palmpona Swap Meet. During the event, Trainers brag about the Pokémon they're seeking to swap in order to generate interest in a trade. All exchanges are processed at transfer portals that are operated by supervisors.

Many other events take place during the week-long festival. Two of the events feature Tauros. The first is the running of the Tauros, where people can prove their bravery and perhaps earn a trophy by touching the horns of a Tauros in a stampeding herd. The other is a battle competition in which Trainers pit their Tauros against each other until a single winner emerges.

The Fire and Rescue Grand Prix is a firefighting competition that pits teams of four Pokémon against each other. Traditionally, the teams are all Water-type Pokémon, but Pokémon of other types have entered the competition.

The events include extinguishing a burning house, a race to retrieve flags by crossing a fire pit on a rope, and the finale in which the top two teams face each other. The contest is a race to retrieve a dummy from a burning building.

Wooper Pond Preschool

When a woman named Olesia discovered a pond between Palmpona and Len Town, she knew it was the perfect place to raise Wooper, and many Wooper agreed with her. As more and more Wooper appeared at her pond, Olesia built a Pokémon Day Care just for them. She studied the small Pokémon and filled a notebook

with information about their care and feeding. Olesia taught the Wooper to follow the beat of a tambourine to help keep them together for their many activities.

WOOPER

Wooper, the Water Fish Pokémon, prefers to live in cold water but forages for food on land. Wooper is the pre-evolutionary form of Quagsire.

Onix Tunnel

The stalagmites and stalactites formed by dripping water may look dangerous, but

your only real concern is the large number of Onix living in the tunnel. The Onix are protective of the tunnel, so you shouldn't go in unless you prepare a way to get past them. Water-type Pokémon are a good choice, but a Jigglypuff is an even better option.

HOUNDOUR

A pack of **Houndour**, the Dark Pokémon, roams the land near an entrance to the Onix Tunnel. Houndour are social creatures that communicate through barking.

Pokémon Circus

A Trainer named Trixie loved the circus as much as she loved Pokémon. When she was old enough, she taught her Pokémon tricks that were best suited to their special abilities, and now they are all performers at this circus that features Pokémon performers.

AZUMARILL

Azumarill, the Aqua Rabbit Pokémon, is one of Trixie's featured performers at their Pokémon circus. Azumarill is the Evolution of Marill. Its large ears allow it to hear great distances, even while underwater.

Ursaring Breeding Grounds

Before you enter this heavily forested area not far from Len Town, look for warning signs that let you know when it's breeding season for Ursaring, the Hibernate Pokemon. If it is breeding season, follow any marked detours and avoid the area. The Ursaring can be dangerous this time of year.

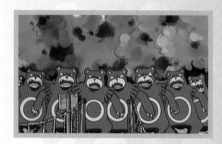

Len Town

Len Town is one of the last stops on your journey from Azalea Town to Goldenrod City. The locals tend to keep Psychic-type Pokémon with them at all times. They're the best form of protection against the Ghost-type Pokémon that have filled the woods around Len Town for hundreds of years.

GIRAFARIG

One of the less common Psychic-type Pokémon found in Len Town is **Girafarig**, the Long Neck Pokémon. Its second head is on its tail, and it has been known to snap at anyone approaching it unaware.

GOLDENROD CITY

If you're not used to crowded cities, your first visit to Goldenrod City will be overwhelming. It's a humongous metropolis that's difficult to navigate due to its many dead end streets. The tunnels under Goldenrod City can be used as shortcuts, but only if you know where you're going. However, it's easy to get turned around and end up farther away from your destination than when you started!

The city is filled with attractions, such as the Goldenrod Radio Tower, the Goldenrod Galleria, and an amazing underground shopping arcade. The main attraction for Pokémon Trainers is, of course, the Goldenrod Gym.

Miltank Dairy

Do you want a chance to scout Whitney, the Goldenrod Gym Leader, before facing her in a Gym battle? Visit the dairy just outside Goldenrod City. It's run by her uncle, Milton. One of Whitney's strongest Pokémon is a Miltank from his dairy.

Goldenrod Gym

This Pokémon Gym is exactly what you'd expect to find in a large city. The exterior is topped by a red dome, and closely resembles sports venues used by professional athletic teams.

Despite its large seating capacity, the battle arena's stadium seating arrangement means even the spectators in the highest rows have a good view of the action.

WHITNEY

Whitney is a kind person who will go out of her way to help lost strangers in her hometown. Unfortunately, despite being a longtime Goldenrod City resident, she isn't as familiar with the shortcuts through the underground shopping arcade as she believes!

None of that means you should underestimate her in a Pokémon battle. Whitney is a top-notch Trainer with a trio of formidable Pokémon. If you do manage to win, your prize is the Plain Badge.

WHITNEY'S POKÉMON

Unlike previous Trainers, Whitney uses three different types of Pokémon. **Miltank**, a Normal-type Pokémon, is Whitney's best battler. It may know multiple moves, but its Rollout attack is usually enough to take out most challengers. **Clefairy** is a Fairy-type Pokémon with the Metronome move. **Nidorina,** Whitney's Poison-type Pokémon, uses Poison Sting and Tackle.

GOLDENROD CITY TO ECRUTEAK CITY

If you were assigning nicknames for the routes between Gym locations, the stretch from Goldenrod City to Ecruteak City could be called a trail of events. There are competitions for specific Pokémon breeds, contests for certain types of Pokémon, and a Pokémon beauty contest.

BLUE MOON FALLS CELEBRATION

Johto's National Park, not far from Goldenrod City, is home to a Bug-type Pokémon catching contest, which is restricted to Trainers under the age of 16. The winner of the contest is awarded a Sun Stone and is allowed to keep the Pokémon he or she catches.

Each participant can use one of his or her own Pokémon to help catch a Bug-type Pokémon in the park. Contestants are also given a special Park Ball that they turn in when they feel they have captured a winning Pokémon.

SUDOWOODO

To settle a debate about what type of Pokémon **Sudowoodo**, the Imitation Pokémon, was, two scientists searched for a specimen near a river close to the national park. After finding and studying one, they concluded Sudowoodo was a Rock-type Pokémon.

Ruins of Alph

Visiting the Ruins of Alph requires a detour away from the shortest path between

Goldenrod City and Ecruteak City, but it's worth the extra time! It is an important archaeological site where the fossils of many prehistoric Pokémon have been discovered. So far, the digging has uncovered fossils of Aerodactyl, Omanyte, and Omastar.

Dr. Anna's Medical Clinic

If you were asked to list locations to receive great medical care, no one would blame you for overlooking an imposing castle at the top of a ridge. However, Dr. Anna's medical clinic is located inside a castle left to her by a patient, and it uses Pokémon to help diagnose and treat injuries. Examples include Spinarak using

its webs as bandages, Zubat's supersonic sound waves acting like an ultrasound machine, and Mareep's electricity running a low-voltage muscle stimulator.

Fighting-type Pokémon Dojo

Kenzo, the shihan of the dojo, instructs his students and their Fighting-type Pokémon in the traditional ways of battle. While training his students, he has also started teaching his granddaughter, Chigusa, everything she needs to know to be his successor when he decides to retire.

AIPOM

In normal circumstances, a hot springs means it's time to relax. At a hot springs not far from Bonitaville, however, you must watch out for a troop of **Aipom**, the Long Tail Pokémon. These Aipom aren't dangerous, but their mischievous antics may leave you feeling annoyed.

SEAKING CATCHING COMPETITION

You can use any type of rod, reel, or lure to catch as many Seaking as possible within the time limit. You can also register one Pokémon to help capture your Seaking.

Only your best Seaking may be entered into the contest, and it must be caught with a special Lake Ball. The contestant with the heaviest Seaking wins a trophy and a year's supply of chocolate bars.

POKÉMON BEAUTY CONTEST

The Pokémon Beauty Contest in Bonitaville requires another detour off the shortest route between Goldenrod City and Ecruteak City, but it's one that all Pokémon breeders will want to make.

The contest is open to any Pokémon, which are judged on their health, their beauty, and how well they have been raised by their breeder. The winning Pokémon is awarded the title "Beauty of the Year."

LEDIAN

The paths through the mountains on the road to Ecruteak City are watched over by the Mountain Patrol and their Pokémon, which includes **Ledian**, the Five Star Pokémon. Trainers and Pokémon must both complete specialized training in order to become full members of the Mountain Patrol.

Wobbuffet Village

Wobbuffet Village is home to the annual Wobbuffet Festival, which celebrates all things Wobbuffet. All visitors are welcomed at Wobbuffet Village, especially Trainers with a Wobbuffet. The people of the village honor their town's namesake by never starting a fight. Just don't think of them as pushovers! They have no problems defending themselves when attacked, just like Wobbuffet using the Counter move.

Pokémon Jujitsu Academy

Many young Trainers bring their Pokémon to this academy to study the principles of Pokémon Jujitsu. There are three types of classes the students can take, and each type has a uniform color assigned to it. Students studying battle techniques wear red. The students in the technical class that makes attacks more effective wear yellow. The students learning about health and nutrition wear blue. All instructors, regardless of the class they teach, wear green.

ARIADOS

The main Pokémon of the Jujitsu Academy's sensei is an **Ariados**, the Long Leg Pokémon. He uses Airados to aid his tutoring of advanced students.

THE GRASS TOURNAMENT

Taking place within a village in a mountain range next to Ecruteak City, this tournament is exclusively for

Trainers of Grass-type Pokémon. The winner receives a victory trophy and a collection of Leaf Stones.

PICHU

Pichu, the Tiny Mouse Pokémon, is the pre-evolutionary form of Pikachu. A wild population of Pichu was caught stealing from an apple orchard outside Ecruteak City. Instead of chasing them away, the orchard's owner trained them to protect the trees and help harvest the apples.

ECRUTEAK CITY

There are two Tin Towers in Ecruteak City, both of which are hundreds of years old. Visiting Pokémon Trainers often mistake the burned tower for the Ecruteak Gym, but all they find are Ghost-type Pokémon that have taken up residence.

The first Tin Tower was a special place where Ho-oh, a Legendary Pokémon, made contact with humans. The Tower was burned when an invading army tried to claim the power of Ho-oh. The people of Ecruteak City built a new Tin Tower, hoping Ho-oh would return to a new place of peace.

Ecruteak Gym

Like much of Ecruteak City, the Gym's exterior has a traditional, rustic look. The arena was not designed for large crowds to watch Pokémon Gym battles. There are no seats or bleachers for spectators. Anyone who wants to watch must stand against a wall.

MORTY

Morty is a descendant of the family that built and maintained the Tin Towers. He is well-known to the wild Ghost-type Pokémon that inhabit the Burned Tower and has learned to understand some of what they say.

As Gym Leader, he is as focused on teaching his students about Ghost-type Pokémon as he is training his own Pokémon. He stresses the importance of disabling opposing Pokémon by confusing or frightening them, because most Ghost-type Pokémon lack physical power. You earn the Fog Badge after defeating Morty in a Gym battle.

MORTY'S POKÉMON

Morty uses a trio of Ghost- and Poison-type Pokémon for Gym battles, all of which are Evolutions of Gastly. Morty's **Gastly** uses Night Shade and Lick. **Haunter** knows the Mean Look, Hypnosis, Lick, Confusion, and Night Shade moves. **Gengar** is the most powerful of the three, and has been observed using Lick, Night Shade, Shadow Ball, and Confusion in battle.

ECRUTEAK CITY TO OLIVINE CITY

Two Gyms are an equal distance from Ecruteak City: Olivine Gym and Mahogany Gym. Where you go next is really up to you, but after so much travel, doesn't a nice day at Olivine City's beach sound good?

MURKROW

The forest just outside Ecruteak City is inhabited by **Murkrow**, the Darkness Pokémon. These flying Pokémon are known to steal shiny objects left unguarded.

Remoraid Mountain

The ruins near Remoraid Mountain are all that is left of the ancient Colossal Tree Tribe, who were humans also known as Remoraidians. The Remoraidians abandoned their home because the river that supplied fresh water dried up after they cut down all the trees to build their city. The area still has not recovered. It's barren except for the ruins, Remoraid fossils, and a Pokémon Center, which survives thanks to an underground water. The normally dried-up Remoraid River briefly flows with a fresh supply of water every 12 years.

RAINBOW LIGHTS AT REMORAID LAKE

At the top of Remoraid Mountain is the empty basin of Remoraid Lake. Brilliant rainbow lights appear above Remoraid Mountain every 12 years, which coincides with the brief flow of water through the normally dry Remoraid River.

The source of the water and lights is the same thing: dozens of Remoraid. The Remoraid return to the lake that bears their name every 12 years, then use a combination of Water Gun and Ice Beam to create a pillar of ice. The ice sparkles in the sunlight to create the rainbow lights, then melts and flows through the river bed.

Sunflora Lodge

Sunflora Lodge is located in an open field at the foot of the mountain range that hosts Snowtop Mountain. The owners are Marcello and Sophia, and they have been married for a long time. The name of the lodge comes from their tradition of including Sunflora in their anniversary photographs. If you stay at the lodge, expect Sophia to share a romantic story. Just be warned that her stories aren't always true!

Snowtop Mountain

While Snowtop Mountain does not have the tallest peak in Johto, it is the location of the highest Pokémon Center: Snowtop Peak. The Snowtop Peak Pokémon Center is also known for its statue of the legendary Pokémon, Articuno. The statue was brought to the Pokémon Center more than one thousand years ago by three travelers who were stranded on the mountain. They claimed Articuno led them to safety and they wanted to express their gratitude.

SWINUB

Local entrepreneurs have trained their **Swinub**, the Pig Pokémon, to sniff out buried hot springs. The Trainers are hired by hot springs companies to discover new locations for resorts.

SUMO CONFERENCE

An intriguing little village between Ecruteak City and Olivine City is home to the Pokémon Sumo Society. Most of these Pokémon Trainers are interested in sumo wrestling, so they train their Pokémon in a similar way.

During the Sumo Conference, Pokémon battles are limited to contests of physical strength and technique. No other attacks or abilities are allowed. Competitors must weigh at least 80 kilograms to enter, and the winner earns a King's Rock and a year's supply of Pokémon food.

Whitestone

Whitestone is one of the most historic sites in Johto. Centuries ago, the citizens of Whitestone began painting the city's buildings white, and the tradition continues to this day. The white paint made the buildings appear to be made from marble.

SMEARGLE

A famous painter named Jack Pollockson tries to live quietly in Whitestone, but his three **Smeargle,** the Painter Pokémon, make that difficult. They use their tails to paint the walls, much to the displeasure of the other people in the city. The color of paint from their tails changes between blue, red, and yellow, to match their current mood.

POKÉMON STREET PERFORMER FESTIVAL

One day each year, Trainers journey to a small town in Johto to show off the skills of their Pokémon at the Street Performer Festival. The skills on display aren't used for battle. Instead, the Pokémon show off other abilities, such as Cubone juggling, a stilt-walking Aipom, Machoke's feats of strength, and a fortune-telling Natu.

HOT AIR BALLOON COMPETITION

If you want to win the Hot Air Balloon competition, you must reach a target and throw a marker into a target on the ground from at least one thousand feet in the air. There is a time limit to the race, so you're allowed to use one Pokémon to help maneuver your balloon. The latest contest featured a high-tech balloon engine going to the winner of the race.

Lake Lucid

Waste from a nearby factory had polluted
Lake Lucid so badly, even the Muks stayed
away! It took three generations of Nurse Joys
to study the effects of the pollution, then
design projects to clean the lake. When the
lake was purified and Water-type Pokémon
returned to it, a Pokémon Center was built
to care for them. Today, the Lake Lucid
Pokémon Center is famous among Trainers
who specialize in Water-type Pokémon.

SEASONAL BOOKS

The grandmother of the current Nurse Joy wrote
the book A *Spring Without Pokémon*, and her
mother wrote a *Summer of Muk*. *Nurse* Joy has
begun work on her own book, *An Autumn Harvest
of Pokémon*.

OLIVINE CITY

In addition to a Pokémon Gym, there's also a Battle Tower located inside Olivine City. To enter the Battle Tower, you must show off your Gym badges to the security guards. If you don't have them, you aren't allowed in!

Shining Lighthouse

Since Olivine City is also a port, a lighthouse is a necessity for warning ships when the area is blanketed by fog. There are two lighthouses in Olivine City. A newer, modern one that uses electricity, and the original, known as the Shining Lighthouse, which uses light reflected from the tail of Ampharos as a warning beacon. Myron, the caretaker of the original lighthouse, is the grandfather of Olivine Gym's Leader, Jasmine.

Olivine Gym

Olivine Gym is a smallish building that looks like a modern recreation of a portion of a pagoda. The battle arena takes up most of the Gym's interior. It is an open space with little room for spectators. You earn the Mineral Badge for defeating Olivine Gym's Leader.

JASMINE

In addition to her duties as Olivine Gym's Leader, Jasmine, with help from her grandfather, runs the Shining Lighthouse. She cares deeply for her Pokémon, especially the Ampharos that provides light for the lighthouse. She has postponed Gym battles in the past when it fell ill, despite the fact she doesn't use it in battle. Her concern for Pokémon does not carry over to opponents faced in battle.

JASMINE'S POKÉMON

Jasmine's **Ampharos** is named Sparkle. An Electric-type, Sparkle supplies the light for the Shining Lighthouse and isn't usually involved in battles. In Gym battles, expect to see **Magnemite**, an Electric- and Steel-type Pokémon that uses Thunderwave. When it's time to get serious, Jasmine chooses **Steelix**, an enormous Steel- and Ground-type Pokémon. When Steelix appears for battle, it uses the Crunch, Iron Tail, Sandstorm, and Dig moves.

CIANWOOD CITY

Travel between Olivine City and Cianwood City is typically uneventful since the two port cities are linked by an express ferry. Beyond the Gym, there is a respected medicine maker who calls Cianwood City home.

Cianwood Gym

You may miss the entrance to Cianwood Gym if you aren't careful. It blends in with the buildings around it, so don't be embarrassed to ask a local for help. The arena lacks proper seating, but there's enough space on the wooden floor for students and their Pokémon to watch battles.

Before or after your battle, prepare for generous portions of special food. The wife of the Gym leader is known to prepare Pokémon Power Food, a nutritious meal designed to strengthen Trainers and Pokémon alike.

CHUCK

He considers himself the meanest, leanest,
toughest, roughest Fighting-type Pokémon
Trainer in all the land, but you can call
him Chuck. Despite his gruff exterior and
obsession with training, Chuck is adored by
his students and he takes his wife's teasing in
stride.

Chuck doesn't do anything halfway. Whether
it's training, eating, teaching, or battling, he puts all his effort into every action. Cianwood
Gym battles are between two Pokémon. If you defeat Chuck, you earn the Storm Badge.

CHUCK'S POKÉMON

Machoke, a Fighting-type Pokémon, is both Chuck's training
partner and primary battler. Machoke uses the Karate Chop,
Submission, and Cross Chop moves in battles. **Poliwrath** is a
Water- and Fighting-type Pokémon that knows Double Slap,
and Water Gun.

ECRUTEAK CITY TO MAHOGANY TOWN

The second Gym that's not far from Ecruteak City is in Mahogany Town. While the road between them winds through valleys and under a mountain, it's an overall quieter route than the one to Olivine City.

Eggseter

In a valley not far from Ecruteak City is a town called Eggseter. Because of its fresh air and perfect soil, it's an ideal location for Pokémon Day Care centers, run by people who call themselves Nesters. Every year, Eggseter hosts a Pokémon Competition. The final event of the competition is an Extreme Pokémon Race.

EXTREME POKÉMON RACE

Extreme Pokémon, where a Pokémon pulls a Trainer riding on a skateboard, is the most popular sport in Eggseter. Every year, the Extreme Pokémon Race draws Trainers and spectators from all around.

You must choose a single Pokémon to use for the entire race. There is no set route to follow during the race, but each competitor must pick up a dummy Pokémon Egg from the Shelby Ranch and return with it to the finish line. The first Trainer to complete the course wins the Gold Poké Ball Trophy.

XATU

The citizens in a town between Eggseter and Mahogany Town rely on **Xatu**, the Mystic Pokémon, to predict the weather, even though their forecasts aren't always accurate. Xatu is the Evolution of Natu.

Lake Rage

Lake Rage is in a heavily forested area close to Mahogany Town. It is off the main road to Mahogany Town, so the people who end up here are usually trying to find a shortcut but take a wrong turn. Be careful if you decide to explore the lake's shoreline. There's a damaged Team Rocket base there.

PROJECT R

Project R was the attempt by Team Rocket's Sebastian and Tyson to modify radio waves into an Evolution-inducement wave, to manipulate Pokémon Evolution. Its headquarters were disguised as a farmhouse near Lake Rage. Early experiments caused nearby Pokémon to become ill. Before the project could be completed, Lance shut it down with help from Pokémon Trainers.

LANCE

Lance is the undisputed champion of the Elite Four, and a Dragonite Trainer. He's also a member of the Pokémon G-Men. The Pokémon G-Men travel the countryside investigating anyone who abuses Pokémon; they work with Officer Jenny to arrest any offenders.

MAHOGANY TOWN

A river runs through Mahogany Town, which is not too far from Lake Rage. Mahogany Town boasts a Gym. The town was also the location of a Team Rocket secret base, which was uncovered when they tried to capture a red Gyrados, but instead let it loose in the nearby river.

Mahogany Gym

With its rounded roof, the Mahogany Gym looks like a converted airplane hangar. Because Pryce, the Gym's Leader, prefers Ice-type Pokémon, he's created a cold area inside the Gym.

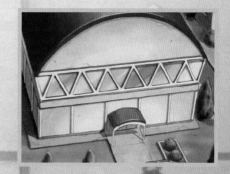

The Gym's battle arena is also cold. Other than a pool of water in the center of the battlefield, the rest of the floor is iced over. When you face Pryce for the Glacier Badge, your two Pokémon must be able to handle a slippery surface.

PRYCE

Pryce is older than the typical Gym Leader. In his youth, he was a successful Trainer with a powerful Piloswine at his side. He defeated all challengers until meeting a Magmar in a national competition. The Magmar left both Pryce and Piloswine injured.

When Piloswine vanished after its injury, Pryce felt abandoned and began to believe that humans and Pokémon should not be friendly. Because of this attitude, and his specialization with Ice-type Pokémon, he was given the nickname Icy Pryce. Pryce was recently reunited with Piloswine after a number of years apart and his attitude regarding friendships with Pokémon has thawed.

PRYCE'S POKÉMON

Dewgong, a Water and Ice-type Pokémon, uses Ice Beam, Aurora Beam, and Headbutt in battle. **Piloswine** is an Ice- and Ground-type Pokémon that knows the Blizzard, Rest, Fury Attack, and Take Down moves.

MAHOGANY TOWN TO BLACKTHORN CITY

Johto's eighth and final official Gym is located in Blackthorn City. The terrain between Mahogany Town and Blackthorn City is a familiar mix of forest and mountainous areas, but also includes a stretch of volcanoes and hot springs. You won't find many towns or cities in this portion of Johto, which means there are almost no contests or competitions to keep you from reaching Blackthorn City in a timely manner.

BELLOSSOM

While you've likely encountered **Bellossom**, the Flower Pokémon, in Johto previously, the Bellossom just outside Mahogany Town are notable for their territorial conflicts with other Grass-type Pokémon in the area.

MAGCARGO

An area of volcanoes and hot springs not far from Mahogany Town is home to a group of wild **Magcargo**, the Lava Pokémon, including one exceptionally large specimen. Magcargo is the Evolution of Slugma.

A Mysterious, Electric Lake

Rumors have swirled about the existence of an almost impossible to find lake in a forest between Mahogany Town and Maroon Town that rejuvenates and restores exhausted and injured Electric-type Pokémon. While not always a reliable source, local folklore claims that the lake's powers come from a sunken temple and a crystal that is recharged by visits from the Legendary Pokémon, Zapdos.

IGGLYBUFF

A city between Mahogany Town and the Slowpoke Temple is the home of Brittany and her pair of **Igglybuff**, the Balloon Pokémon. Igglybuff is the pre-evolutionary form of Jigglypuff. Brittany is the host of an eponymous television show, but she claims no one watched it until she put her twin Igglybuff on the program.

Lake Enlightenment

This lake is known as both Lake Enlightenment and Lake Slowpoke. It is called Lake Enlightenment because it's close to a spot where a priest once achieved enlightenment. The Lake Slowpoke name comes from the Slowpoke that ponder existence on the lake's shore while fishing with their tails.

Slowpoke Temple

Slowpoke Temple was built on the spot where a priest achieved enlightenment while meditating among Slowpoke hundreds of years ago. At the heart of the temple is a giant, golden Slowpoke statue.

The temple's name comes from the Slowpoke that have lived in the area for many generations. Despite its age, thousands of people and Pokémon journey to the temple every year. Students at Slowpoke Temple dedicate their lives to pondering the meaning of existence, just like a Slowpoke.

Maroon Town

Maroon Town is a nice place to stop on the road between Mahogany Town and Blackthorn City. It's a quiet town with a radio station you can tune into if you want to catch up on the news. It's also known for having one of the best hamburgers in Johto.

POKÉMON MYSTERY CLUB

Although the Pokémon Mystery Club, or PMC, claims to be a worldwide network of investigators, the only known members are Ken and Mary. Their primary interest is proving that some Pokémon have extraterrestrial origins.

They take offense when they are compared to Team Rocket, and they scoff at Team Rocket's methods. PMC also has access to better technology than that which Team Rocket uses. Unfortunately, they do share Team Rocket's view on Pokémon ownership: any Pokémon you catch in a net belongs to you.

CLEFFA

One of the Pokémon the PMC investigate is **Cleffa**, the Star Shape Pokémon. The pre-evolutionary form of Clefairy is of special interest to the PMC due to their belief that Cleffa arrive on Earth riding shooting stars.

Battle Park

The Battle Park is a popular destination among Trainers looking for challenging battles for their Pokémon. At the Battle Park, you can choose the Pokémon you want to challenge, as well as the environment of the battleground. The Battle Park has almost every Pokémon there is.

The park is run by professional Trainers. The Pokémon from the park are powerful and also obedient when they are inside the park. If anyone forgets to return, or tries to steal, a Pokémon from the Battle Park, the Pokémon will refuse to obey and then return to the park immediately.

BLACKTHORN CITY

Long ago, according to legend, a fierce Dragon-type Pokémon terrorized the residents of the area that became Blackthorn City. The city's first Gym Leader defeated it and claimed one of its fangs as a keepsake. The Dragon Fang remains a family treasure that has been kept in Blackthorn Gym since.

PURIFICATION RITUAL

The Dragon Fang must be put through a purification ritual in water from the Blackthorn Lake on a day that comes only once every three years. The purpose of the ritual is to bring peace and happiness to all Dragon-type Pokémon.

Dragon's Den

The Dragon's Den is a complex maze of tunnels that connects Blackthorn Lake and the Dragon Holy Land. The tunnels are said to have been created by dragons hundreds of years ago.

Dragon Holy Land

The Dragon Holy Land is a grassy meadow surrounded by sheer rock cliffs. Thousands of Pokémon of all types live peacefully in the Dragon Holy Land, and all the flowers in the Dragon Holy Land remain in bloom all year.

The Dragonite that protects the Pokémon of the land was the Pokémon of the first Blackthorn Gym Leader. The Trainer loved the Dragon Holy Land more than anything. He dedicated his whole life to preserving and protecting it. Dragonite continues the work, carrying on in the spirit of the Gym Leader, but it has never been the same since its Trainer passed on.

DRAGON SHRINE AND PRAYER FLAME

The vault-like structure on the lakeshore in the Dragon Holy Land is the Dragon Shrine. In the past, when people considered Pokémon to be enemies, the Dragon Shrine was built as a symbol of hope that humans and Pokémon could coexist peacefully. When that hope became reality, people constructed the Prayer Flame, which is permanently housed in Dragon Shrine. The Prayer Flame has been burning for 500 years.

Blackthorn Gym

The Blackthorn Gym is an imposing stone building with a red roof. It is the headquarters for all up-and-coming Dragon-type Pokémon Trainers, including Lance of the Elite Four. When you face Gym Leader Clair for the Rising Badge, be ready to battle in multiple environments. The arena has a pool of water in middle, and the roof is retractable. That means you must deal with the fire of Clair's

Dragon-type Pokémon, the water of the pool, and the sky when the roof is opened.

CLAIR

Despite her many responsibilities, Clair is still a kind and caring Gym Leader. Her duties include caring for her Pokémon, running

the Blackthorn City Gym, instructing Dragon-type Pokémon Trainers, and preserving the important elements of Blackthorn City's history, such as performing the purification ritual for the Dragon Fang.

CLAIR'S POKÉMON

Kingdra is a Water- and Dragon-type Pokémon with the Twister, Hydro Pump, Agility, Swift, and Hyper Beam moves. The mighty Gyarados, a Water- and Flying-type Pokémon, has used Hydro Pump, Hyper Beam, Dragon Breath, and Bite in battle. Clair's recently evolved Dragonair is a Dragon-type Pokémon whose moves include Hyper Beam, Dragon Rage, Safeguard, and Iron Tail.

BLACKTHORN CITY TO MT. SILVER

If you're a Pokémon Trainer who just collected your final Gym badge, your next destination is Mt. Silver. Your path will takes you to new areas as well as familiar locations, such as New Bark Town.

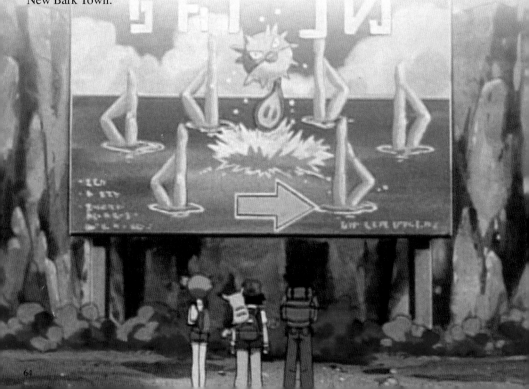

Coastline Gym

While it's an impressive building, the Coastline Gym is not an official Johto Gym. Dorian, the Gym's Leader, hopes to change that by making it more popular. He specializes in Water-type Pokémon and tries to emulate Cerulean Gym.

The Gym's arena is underwater, meaning Trainers must wear special breathing gear for battles. Because Dorian also puts on synchronized swimming shows with his Pokémon—which include Lanturn, Maintine, and Qwilfish—the Coastline Gym has rows and rows of bleachers around its arena.

Pokémon Marine Laboratory

The Pokémon Marine Laboratory is on the coast between Blackthorn City and New Bark Town. Daisy, the lab's director, works in the field of Pokémon marine biology, which studies the living patterns of marine Pokémon. She hopes to apply her studies to improve human life. Daisy uses a submarine, the S.S. Innocent Pearl, to get a closer look at Pokémon life underwater.

SLOWKING

Not far from Mt. Silver, a wall mural that depicts an ancient event was exposed when an earthquake nearly drained a lake bed. A professor and his daughter studied the mural and determined that it detailed how a Slowpoke could evolve into a **Slowking**, the Royal Pokémon, with help from a King's Rock.

Unown Dimension

Unown are mysterious Pokémon that come in a variety of shapes. Legend says Unown can make telepathic contact with humans. Some scientists think Unown come from a different dimension. There have been a few unverified reports of visits to this Unown Dimension, including one from a group of Trainers in Johto who were on their way to Mt. Silver.

MT. SILVER

Mt. Silver is the final destination for Pokémon Trainers after they earn all eight Johto Gym Badges. At the foot of the mountain is Silver Town, home of the Silver Conference. There's also a Pokémon Preservation Center run by Rangers at the heart of a Pokémon preserve on Mt. Silver.

SNEASEL

Mt. Silver is the home of a group of wild **Sneasel**, the Sharp Claw Pokémon. A Sneasel recently terrorized the torch runners at the Ho-Oh Shrine until it was captured by a Trainer named Harrison.

Ho-Oh Shrine and Sacred Flame

The Ho-Oh Shrine was built to honor Ho-Oh ending a war between two human civilizations. Inside the shrine is the Sacred Flame, which has burned since the end of that war hundreds of years ago. As the Silver Conference begins, a runner lights a torch from the Sacred Flame and begins a relay to Silver Stadium. During the Silver Conference's opening ceremonies, the final relay runner takes the torch to light the brazier at the top of the Silver Stadium platform.

Silver Town

Silver Town is the home of Johto's Silver Conference. All Trainers who qualify must sign up for the Silver Conference at the Silver Town Pokémon Center, which is one of the largest Pokémon Centers in the world. Trainers stay in the Athlete's

Village during the Silver Conference. From their rooms, the contestants can access a database to research the other Trainers and their Pokémon.

SILVER CONFERENCE

The Silver Conference is the name of the Johto League championship. The preliminaries for the championship are called the athlete screening round. Trainers select one of their Pokémon for three battles. The top 48 Trainers from athlete screening advance to the semifinals.

For the semifinals, the 48 contestants are organized into blocs of three Trainers. The Trainers battle each other in a 3-on-3, round-robin format. They earn three victory points for a win and one victory point for a draw. The Trainer with the most victory points in each bloc advances to the Victory Tournament.

Matches for the Victory Tournament are held in the Silver Stadium, which features a battlefield that changes between grass, rock, water, and ice. The Victory Tournament is single-elimination. The battles between the 16 Trainers who advanced from the semifinals are full 6-on-6 matches.

WHIRL ISLANDS

If you're a Water-type Pokémon Trainer looking for a challenge, try the Whirl Cup. The Whirl Cup is a competition held once every three years on the Whirl Islands. Trainers from all over the world travel to Johto in order to participate.

If you're interested in something other than Water-type Pokémon, there's still plenty to do in the Whirl Islands. Each island has its own festivals, events, and competitions.

Blue Point Isle

Blue Point Isle is known as the entry point to the Whirl Islands. Its name comes from the large, blue rock that safely guided ancient seamen into port at the end of a long journey.

The largest city on Blue Point Isle is Inland City. If you want to sign up for the Whirl Cup, you can do so at Inland City's Pokémon Center. Other cities include Bluefinland, where you can catch a ferry to Yellow Rock Isle, and Blue Lagoon, which is a special place for Chinchou.

A PARADE FOR THE CHINCHOU

A Chinchou nesting site once at the bottom of the ocean was raised over time by seismological forces until it emerged from the water as part of the Whirl Islands. This nesting site is now under a lake near the present-day city of Blue Lagoon.

Blue Lagoon holds a parade on the day the recently hatched Chinchou leave the lake and head for the ocean. A few townspeople are selected to accompany the Angler Pokémon on their journey, to ensure they reach the ocean safely. The remaining people line the streets and throw water on the Chinchou, so they maintain a high moisture level.

Pudgy Pidgey Isle

Pudgy Pidgey Isle is a small island near the coast of Blue Point Isle, and the home to extremely large Pidgey. Because the whirlpools around the island kept away predators, the Pidgey no longer needed to fly. The Pokémon Protection Agency declared the island a Pidgey reserve, and the large Pidgeys have been studied ever since. There is a human caretaker

on the island named Wilbur who is trying to get the Pidgeys to fly again.

Yellow Rock Isle

Yellow Rock Isle gets its name from the color of the rocks on the island. The locals on Yellow Rock Isle like the color yellow so much, they paved their streets with yellow stone. Yellow Rock Isle relies on many types of Pokémon to power its fishing and farming industries. Ogi City, on the north side of Yellow Rock Isle, is the port for the ferry that runs between Yellow Rock Isle and Red Rock Isle.

PIC CORSOLA

Corsola, the Coral Pokémon, is an import part of life on Yellow Rock Isle. Houses on the coastline are usually built on Corsola nests. When Corsola shed their horns, the people on Yellow Rock Isle turn them into pieces of art.

Red Rock Isle

Red Rock Isle is the home of the Whirl Cup competition. Registration for Whirl Cup preliminaries is done at the Pokémon Center in Scarlet City, which is on the southern coast of Red Rock Isle. The main arena for the Whirl Cup is also in Scarlet City. Transit Town, where you can catch a ferry to either Silver Rock Isle or Olivine City on mainland Johto, is on the northeastern tip of Red Rock Isle.

WHIRL CUP

This prestigious competition for Water-type Pokémon Trainers takes place once every three years. Trainers arrive up to a month before the competition to acclimate their Pokémon to the varied climates of the Whirl Islands. After signing up for the tournament at Inland City's Pokémon Center, all participants receive a rulebook.

The winner of the tournament is awarded a Mystic Water pendant and the title, Water Pokémon Alpha Omega. Whirl Islands legends say that long ago, expert Water-type Pokémon Trainers were known by that name.

SEA PRIESTESS MAYA

The rituals associated with the great traditions of the Whirl Islands are kept vital and alive through the teachings of the Sea Priestess. The name of the current Sea Priestess is Maya. She opens the Whirl Cup with an invocation of the Sea Spirit Union, which brings together the energy from all Water-type Pokémon. At the end of six days of Whirl Cup competition, she presents the winner with their awards.

Diglett Village

The Diglett and Dugtrio of Diglett Village helped
the original villagers turn a desert into fertile
farmland, and helped them cultivate their fields.
The original villagers are now grandparents, but
they refuse to give up working their farmland.
There are reports of a band of Diglett thieves (who
call themselves the Band of Diglett Thieves) in the
area, so be careful when you travel there. Oddly,

there haven't been any reports of the thieves bothering anyone who isn't a long-time resident of
Diglett Village.

Silver Rock Isle

Silver Rock Isle gets its name from the silver rock
stone found only on the island. Silver rock stone is
one of the hardest and most beautiful substances
in the world. Craftsman on the island turn silver
rock stone into jewelry, with a silver wing shape
being the most common. A local legend claims
that wearing jewelry made from silver rock stone
protects one from danger.

Ogi Isle

Ogi Isle is connected to Silver Rock Isle through a cave that runs under the sea. Old stories and legends tell of a mysterious Pokémon living around the island, but no sightings have been confirmed.

LANTURN

Lanturn, the Light Pokémon, is the Evolution of Chinchou. The light that emits from its tentacle-like limb shines brightly enough to illuminate the bottom of a deep sea.

LEGENDARY POKÉMON OF JOHTO

The cities and towns of Johto are filled with folk tales, myths, and stories about five Legendary Pokémon: Entei, Lugia, Ho-Oh, Raikou, and Suicune. While many people know a legend or a myth, a few Pokémon enthusiasts have dedicated themselves to learning more about the Legendary Pokémon.

EUSINE

Eusine is an expert in Pokémon legends from all over the world who researches ancient Pokémon literature. He is also the foremost expert on Suicune, who appears only to the most skilled Pokémon Trainers. His interest in Suicune borders on an obsession.

Morty

Morty, the Ecruteak Gym Leader, is a descendant of the people allowed to meet with Ho-Oh when the original Tin Tower stood. He has been entrusted with the history of Ho-Oh's relationship with the Tin Towers and the Crystal Bells.

Nelson

While less famous than Eusine and Morty, Nelson has been single-mindedly pursuing Entei with the intention of catching it. While he still has not captured an Entei, he refuses to give up his lifelong dream.

LUGIA

Sightings of Lugia are concentrated around the Whirl Islands, in particular Silver Isle and Ogi Isle. Tales of Lugia usually revolve around the Legendary Pokémon rescuing humans caught in bad weather.

The most famous story from the Whirl Islands is many years old. A fishing boat was caught in a violent storm. The ship broke apart and sank, and the sailors were forced overboard into the rough seas. A whirlpool, shining a mysterious bright light, arose and the storm dissipated.

As the skies cleared, a shimmering silver wing fell from the sky. From that day forward, people in the Whirl Islands believe silver, wing-shaped jewelry would protect them and bring good luck. Silver wings remain the most common type of jewelry made from the silver rock stone that gives Silver Rock Isle its name.

HO-OH

Ho-Oh, the Rainbow Pokémon, has strong ties to two cities in Johto. On Mt. Silver, not far from Silver Town, is the Ho-Oh Shrine. It was built to honor Ho-Oh's part in ending a battle that involved humans and Pokémon. Because of the battle, a lake dried up, the land wasted away, and all life in the area disappeared. That was when Ho-Oh appeared and burned all human weapons with a rose-colored flame. From the ashes of that fire, life slowly returned to the lake and the land around it. Once that happened, people put aside their differences and worked together to achieve peace.

Ho-Oh was also known to visit the Tin Tower in Ecruteak City as a sign of peace. The Crystal Bells in the Tin Tower would ring to herald its appearance. Only select people were allowed to meet with Ho-Oh.

Three hundred years ago, a battle for control of Ho-Oh's power spilled into the Tin Tower. A fire was started and the Tin Tower burned. The people of Ecruteak City built a new Tin Tower next to the original, and placed within it all the bells that could be salvaged from the original

tower. Despite their hopes that Ho-Oh would return, there have not been any sightings of the Legendary Pokémon in Ecruteak City since the fire.

ENTEI, RAIKOU, AND SUICUNE

The legend of Ho-Oh described its fierce anger that would only melt away once the hearts of Pokémon and humans finally met as one. To continue to watch the world, Ho-Oh needed help. Drawing from the forces of nature and its own ancient power, Ho-Oh gave new life to three Pokémon caught in the fire started during the battle in the Tin Tower.

The reincarnation of the north wind is Suicune, Entei is the reincarnation of the volcano, and Raiku is the reincarnation of thunder. These three Pokémon remain to observe humans, waiting for the day people and Pokémon live together in cooperation and harmony. Most of the sightings of this trio of Pokémon have been quick glimpses of a figure shrouded in shadows.

Johto Region Field Guide

Written by Ken Schmidt

DK/Prima Games, a division of Penguin Random House LLC
6081 East 82nd Street, Suite #400
Indianapolis, IN 46250

ISBN: 978-0-7440-1970-4

Printing Code: The rightmost double-digit number is the year of the book's printing; the rightmost single-digit number is the number of the book's printing. For example, 18-1 shows that the first printing of the book occurred in 2018.

20 19 18   4 3 2 1

001-313657-February/2019

Printed in China.

CREDITS
Publishing Manager
Tim Cox

Book Designer
Carol Stamile

Production
Beth Guzman

Copy Editor
Tim Fitzpatrick

PRIMA GAMES STAFF
VP
Mike Degler

Licensing
Paul Giacomotto

Marketing Manager
Jeff Barton